Sri Lanka
Travel Guide

- From a Declaration of Principles which was accepted and approved equally by a Committee of the American Bar Association and a Committee of Publishers and Associations.

clarifying purposes only and are the

owned by the owners themselves, not

affiliated with this document.

Table of Contents

Introduction   9

Brief History of Sri Lanka   33

Places to see   39

Colombo   39

Kandy   44

Dambulla   51

Nuwara Eliya   54

Trincomalee   60

Arugam Bay   62

Activities to do in Sri Lanka   65

Enjoy a Cultural Dance   65

Sightsee the Sigiriya Rock Fortress   67

Visit the Tea Plantation & Tea Factory
                                                70

Visit the Strawberry Farms   73

Polonnaruwa City Tour   75

Anuradhapura Sightseeing   76

Hakgala Botanical Gardens   80

Galle City Tour   82

Water Sports in Unawatuna Beach   84

Budurugawala Rock Carvings   87

Turtles Hatchery in Kosgoda   88

Elephants &Wild Life Sanctuary   88

Buddhist Monasteries and Meditation
Centers of Sri Lanka   90

SriLankan Food   98

Things to remember on Your Sri Lankan
Visit   106

Conclusion   110

Introduction

Pristine beaches, sunny weather, cool air and peaceful waters; Sri Lanka has it all and offer much more on a beach holiday. Sri Lanka is an island country that is democratic and is situated in the Indian Ocean in South Asia. Situated below India, Sri Lanka is vulnerable from all sides as it's covered by water. It's covered by Arabian Sea, Bay of Bengal and Indian Ocean on all sides. As a Buddhist country, Sri Lanka has disciplined and polite people. A tourist destination, Sri Lanka offers amazing hospitality to visitors. There are several beaches and coastal areas through out the country, where you can relax and unwind. Most of their beaches are untouched by modernity and offer natural habitats to feel relaxed and stress free on a vacation.

A drop in the ocean, at the foot of the Indian sub-continent, the island of Sri Lanka literally resembles a tear drop. Very much a part of India, till a few thousand years ago, it was here that the battle between the Hindu God Lord Ram and the Lankan king Ravana was fought, after the latter abducted the former's wife and held her captive in Sri Lanka. When Sri Lanka was considered to be a part of India, there were many men and women from the island who traveled to Nalanda University in North India to study. During the pre-Vedic times, Sulabha and Gargi, two women from Lanka are known to have composed the Vedas, at a time when women were accorded equal status in society.

Sri Lanka has experienced the influence of several cultures since time immemorial. The Portuguese, the Dutch and the British have all taken to the land for its spices, as flies to a honey-pot; Lanka being a tropical coast-line and rich in spices. The last to invade were the British, which set up railways and roads.

With the Indian Ocean for company, the island country known as the Pearl of the Indian Ocean looks verdant with numerous palm-fringed coastline dotting the pristine waters. The tropical rainforests are eternally drenched in mist adding to the beauty and romance on a Sri Lanka vacation.

Negombo and Bentota are some of the clean shores. For a romantic rendezvous, head for the cozy Bentota Resort complex. The open-air theatre is an adventure by itself where you can watch mask-dancing, seated under the cool breeze of swaying palms.

A well-developed tourist spot, Hikkaduva is famous for coral-reefs. The main attraction here is a glass-bottom boat that allows a crystal clear view of the reefs that run parallel to the shores.

Heard of 'singing fish'? Head for Batticaloa and witness it yourself. Surrounded by an enormous lagoon, this place is a sight on full-moon nights, when you can hear the sea reverberating with musical vibrations!

Elevated at an altitude of 2000 meters, this is one hill station that no brochure will miss to describe. It's as picturesque as the brochures have painted it. The green slopes filled with tea plantations, with only silver streams gushing forth as demarcations, Nuwara Eliya is picture-perfect in every sense. Even

Pidurutalagala-the highest mountain in Sri Lanka stands tall to catch a glimpse of this beautiful vista!

An 18-hole golf course is another attraction of this colonial hill-station. In the Southwest, are botanical garden Hakgala that is a natural reserve replete with rich flora and fauna.

South of Hakgala, is the highest plateau-the Horton Plains- the emerald soft, green of which are soothing balm to your urban eyes. Nestled within, is a lovely park. The beauty of the plains is so exquisite, that Kirigalpotta and

Thotupola the second and third highest mountains of the country, vie with each other, trying to take a peek at the plains below. The plains are fertile with the land's main rivers- Kelani, Walawe and Mahaweli nourishing it, making it abound with flora and fauna. The Baker Falls with its sparkling silver waterfall completes the scenic view. The Sambar, leopard and wild boars can be spotted here.

As the temperature dips, it's wise to carry warm woolens.

A majestic mountain, the Sri Pada is another quaint hill with verdant forests. It's interesting to note that this place is held sacred by the world's four important faiths-Hindus, Buddhists, Christians and Muslims. Also known as Samanalakande, (butterfly mountain), the place is inhabited by countless pretty, dainty butterflies, in myriad hues and designs. You get a beautiful view of the hill from the sea below. Watching the sun rise, while sipping your first cuppa, can be an enchanting experience.

Adam's peak is considered a holy mountain; one can find pilgrims trudging uphill from December to April. Regardless of one's religious inclinations, trekkers trek upwards only in the hope of catching the sun rise-one of the finest in Asia! Dotted with many refreshment stalls, that are all aglow during nightfall, the mountain at night resembles a miniature stairway heading straight from the earth heavenwards!

Trail of Buddhism is still apparent, as the land abounds with Stupas spanning from Emperor Ashoka's times. The 12th century statues of Lord Buddha, carved from single granite stone, in Polonnaruwa is one of the finest in Sri Lanka. One of the sculptures in Buduruvagala is a standing Buddha statue which measures 51 feet from head to toe.

Independence Memorial Hall, White Buddha, Temple of Tooth Relic, Peradeniya Royal Botanical garden, Pinnawela Elephant Orphanage, Maha Bodhi tree and Jetawanaramaya are a must see.

Sri Lankan cuisine is mostly sea food along with rice. Coconuts are liberally used in their dishes. It'll be unique to taste aromatic foods that are available only here as rare spices are used in them. Tea is one of the important drinks here. Sri Lankan Green tea is world famous and the aromatic brew has many health benefits.

Sri Lankan music and dance are elegant and peppy numbers. Beach festivals are a rage here. With wining, dining and dancing you will have no complaints about a holiday to this amazing island.

The choice of where to go and what to see is endless and your trip may seem insufficient trying to catch everything from dazzling temples to forts of World Heritage, from vibrant resort towns to timeless rural settlements and from national parks where natural wildlife is untouched to exotic beaches. You have it all here.

Adventurous options like trekking on mountainous jungle terrain either on foot or elephant back, white water rafting and a four wheel safari ride will quench your thirst for thrill, enthusiasm and dare devils. Sri Lanka's extensive coast line beckons each of its visitors, offering rich and relaxing joys of beach life like scuba diving, sailing and canoeing only after you're trained by experienced experts. The revitalizing and rejuvenation massage is one of key secrets to its popularity and you can feel at home at any one of the famous and luxurious spas. Sri Lankan cuisine is considered as one of the worlds healthiest and most delicacies in Asia. It is also a shopper's paradise with gleaming modern malls selling leading brands and giant markets where you can really feel the essence of Sri Lanka's diverse culture. Local fashions and handicrafts at give away prices may leave you penniless but happy with a feeling of value for money.

How to Reach

Sri Lanka is connected through air and water ways. It has an international airport that is connected to the Western world. From USA and UK you can take a direct British Airways flight or Sri Lankan Airlines to reach Bandaranaike international airport in Katunayake, in Sri Lanka. There are direct flights from India, Malaysia, Singapore, Hongkong and Thailand as well.

You can also cruise from India and Singapore to Sri Lanka. It depends upon your vacation plans and if you like sailing. There are luxury liners and cruise ships to Colombo, the capital of Sri Lanka.

Visa Regulations

Getting a tourist visa to Sri Lanka is very easy. You can get it from their website. Any nationality can apply for a tourist visa on the Sri Lankan website and get it within a day or two. Sometimes you get it instantly as well. The tourist visa issued is valid for 30 days. People residing in Singapore, Seychelles and Maldives are exempt from getting a visa. They can simply arrive for a vacation. There is a small fee levied for acquiring a tourist visa to Sri Lanka. It is around $30-$35. All you need is a passport with 6 months validity.

Currency

Sri Lankan Rupee (LKR) is the currency of this island country. The Sri Lankan Rupee is equal to –

1 Indian Rupees = 2.53 LKR

1 USA Dollar = 175 LKR (Sri Lankan rupees)

1 British Pound = 228.62 LKR

1 Euro = 197 LKR

Master card and Visa cards are accepted in all major hotels and establishments. It is better to carry cash also as you may need to pay at the beaches and for local food. There are international outlets (food joints) in cities like Colombo where you can pay using Master/ Visa card. You can also exchange currency at any bank in Colombo or other major cities. American dollar and British pounds and Euro are widely accepted everywhere.

Best time to visit

Sri Lanka lies in the equatorial region. Though Sri Lanka is a small country the weather patterns vary from the East coast to West coast. The island country faces two monsoons. The first monsoon appears between May and August known as the Yala Monsoon. This lashes the South and West coast. At this time the air travel and accommodation prices are pretty low.

The season from April to September is ideal to visit this beautiful beach country. You can visit the East coast.

The weather is cool and sunny as well. The peak tourist season is between December and March. The southern coast is busiest at this time of the year.

The best time to visit the west and south coasts and hill country is from December to March, while the best weather on the east coast is from April to September. There are beach cottages where you can literally live in the beach and enjoy sunshine, sand and sleep.

What to wear?

Light and cool cotton clothes are ideal for a Sri Lankan vacation. The people here are conservative and traditional. Pack modest swim wear and several shrugs and jackets to cover your body. Sarongs will be stylish as well as cover you. Carry sun tan lotion, glares and moisturizers with you.

Sinhalese, Tamil and English are the widely spoken languages in Sri Lanka.

Vaccinations

For tourists the usually recommended vaccinations for Sri Lanka include cover against the childhood diseases (Tetanus, Diphtheria and Poliomyelitis, Measles, Mumps and Rubella) as well as cover against food and water borne diseases of Typhoid and Hepatitis A.

Brief History of Sri Lanka

Legend has it that King Ravana was a demon king who abducted Sita, the beautiful wife of Lord Rama from India and took her to Sri Lanka. He held her captive there till her husband went to war, killed him and brought her back. Later Ravana's younger brother Vibheeshana was crowned the king and he maintained good relations with Indian rulers. Even today in South India there is a temple where Vibheeshana's descendants get first respect to perform rituals to the God. In the 5th century BC immigrants from Northern

India arrived in Sri Lanka and settled there. The first Sinhalese kingdom was formed by King Vijaya around Anuradhapura with just a few hundred people.

The Portuguese occupied Sri Lanka in 1500 and gave it the name Ceilao. The Sri Lankans fought for independence and won against the Portuguese. Around 1800's the British occupied Sri Lanka for their abundant spices, coffee and tea plantations. They changed the name to Ceylon from Ceilao. The British took several workers from India to work in the coffee and tea plantations as laborers. These people settled there and made Ceylon their home. After independence from the British rule Ceylon changed its name to Sri Lanka. Sri Lanka has fought two wars to maintain their independent status.

There is actually a bridge built by Lord Rama between Rameshwaram in South India to Sri Lanka. Presently it is submerged under water. It is believed that a tsunami or earthquake would've separated Sri Lanka from India and made it into an island surrounded by water on all sides.

Sri Lanka became a Buddhist country when emperor Ashoka of the Maurya dynasty spread his kingdom to this island region. His son and daughter became the peace carriers and converted everyone to Buddhism after a tragic war. Ashoka himself turned into a Buddhist monk after seeing the dead bodies of innocent people killed in the war.

There are several Buddhist monasteries and one of the largest Buddha statues is situated in Anuradhapura. Sri Lankan Tamils and

Sinhalese live in harmony and prey to Buddha.

In places like Jaffna and Trincomalee there are Tamilians who've migrated from India. They're known as Sri Lankan Tamils. In eastern part of Sri Lanka refugees from Burma settled there and made their home. The Sri Lankans follow matriarchal style of life. The women are dominant and they take important decisions in the family. Though Sri Lanka's culture, food and ethnicity is similar to India, they're independent and different in many ways. Sri Lanka is rich and vibrant in culture, history and heritage. It has amazing stories to tell and you'll not be disappointed visiting this magnificent country on a vacation.

Good food, leisurely lifestyle, water sports, lazy walks, mountain trails and splendid wine; what more can you ask for from a beach vacation?

Now let us take a look at some of the activities you can do to enjoy and have a memorable vacation in this beautiful island country.

Places to see
Colombo

Colombo is the capital city of Sri Lanka. Dotted with swanky skyscrapers and modern technology the infrastructure is no less than any other top city in the world. The British and Portuguese architecture is aesthetically imbibed into modern buildings, high rises and shopping malls. Some of the important spots to see in the city are the giant Buddha statue in Gangaramaya temple, National Museum of Colombo where you can find Sri Lankan history, the red mosque, Dutch museum and

Pettah, etc. Shopping can be exciting here. Handloom fabrics, colorful ceramics, antiques, leather products and jewelry are a must buy from Colombo. The clock tower in the fort area is a must see too.

Also enjoy a tuk tuk ride on a three wheeler. This open rickshaw is popular to travel here. It may cost you around $15 to go on a tour of temples, lunch and refreshments. Bargain well and enjoy a ride.

Galle Face Green promenade is the best place to take a morning/ evening walk. On the banks of the Indian Ocean you can enjoy a peaceful stroll by the open sea and taste some of the best local street food. Crabs, shrimp on lentil cakes is a delicacy you should relish here.

Bu Ba beach restaurant at mount Lavinia is the best for sea food and Nana's are the best for street food.

Upali's in Colombo serve authentic Sri Lankan food of rice and curry. The cost is negligible.

The Grand Oriental Hotel is the best place to enjoy pre dinner drinks and cocktails. Built in 1920 this hotel has still preserved its old world charm. The view is breathtaking while you sip on their wine, local arrack or gin & tonic. The cost is hardly anything. Drink here and then proceed elsewhere to eat.

The Ministry of Crab is a fine dining restaurant just close to Grand Oriental Hotel. You can relish chilli crab and crabzilla as much as you want.

Shangri La Hotel in Colombo is the best place for grilled food and is attached with a bar as well. Tomahawk steak is delicious here. It may cost you around

$180 per night at Shangri La Hotel. You can use your international credit cards here.

There are several budget hotels and motels available here.

Kandy

Kandy is one of the most architectural and religious city of the island country. It is set on a plateau surrounded by hills and mountain ranges. These mountain ranges are bio-diverse rain forests and also are home to vast expanse of tea gardens. The greenery turns dark and plush during monsoons and the smoky mountains look majestic and tall during a cloudy day. Trekking in these slopes can be fun.

Kandy Lake

In the heart of the city is the Kandy Lake that was artificially made in 1807 by King Vikrama Rajasinghe. This lake is also known as the sea of milk. Surrounding by hills and trees the lake is a beautiful place to watch the sunset. There is also a jogging track adjacent to it. Tranquil, charming and peaceful the lake depicts the nature of Sri Lankans. You cannot miss the lake as it is in the middle of the city. You can enjoy the birds chirping, the tall palm trees swishing in the wind and other enchanting sounds of nature here. Kandy Lake is a scenic splendor.

Temple of Sacred Tooth Relic

Adjacent to the Kandy Lake is the Temple of Sacred Tooth. Sri Dalada Maligawa also known as Sacred Tooth Temple is a Buddhist relic that was built in the 1600's. Buddha's tooth relic has been preserved here. The Sri Lankans worship it as Buddha is their deity. It is located inside the royal palace of Kandy King. This is a world heritage site.

Royal botanical garden

The royal Botanical garden situated in Peradeniya, West of Kandy is one of the largest gardens in Asia. They house rare orchids that are unique to this place. The flora and fauna attracts more than 2 million visitors annually to this garden. The amazing array of palms and imposing variety of tropical woody plants is a must see. You'll need a half a day to stroll through the entire garden. They close by 6 PM.

Visit spices and tea factories – Situated very close to the botanical gardens is the tea and spices garden in Peradeniya. You can see, smell and taste a variety of spices and teas that you'll not find anywhere else. The spices and tea was the reason Portuguese, Dutch and British invaded Sri Lanka. You visit the factories and see how they're made and buy them too.

Kandy to Ella train journey

Experience a train journey through tall mountains, deep valleys, surrounded by tea gardens and coffee estates. Kandy to Ella is a scenic marvel and your vacation will be incomplete if you don't experience this beautiful train journey. It is a 7 hour stunning and picturesque trip that will leave you enchanted and thrilled. The panoramic view is ideal for photography. You can hang out of the train to capture nature at its best. Since it is a hilly terrain the train moves slowly. This train journey is popular and always booked. You need to book in advance so that you can get reserved seats.

If you wish to avoid the rush, take a tuk tuk to Peradeniya and take the train coming from Colombo to Kandy. All the trains stop here. Most of the passengers get down here, so it'll be easy to get seats before the train reaches Kandy.

Dambulla

Situated exactly in the heart of Sri Lanka, Dambulla is in the middle of the country. Due to its strategic positioning between Colombo and Kandy, Dambulla distributes vegetables to the entire country. Dambulla is well known for rose quartz mountain range and iron wood forests known as Na Uyana Aranya. Aranya in Sanskrit means forest. Its strategic position enables you to visit any part of Sri Lanka. It is also famous for its cave temple that is beautiful and magnificent. There are more than 80 caves in the surrounding areas. Out of them 5 caves contains paintings and statues that talk about Gods and Goddesses like Buddha, Vishnu and Ganesh. Buddha's life and times have been depicted in detail here. This archeological site has historical importance and gives a peak into the Indian influence that is evident in the island country. Popham's Arboretum, Buddhist Museum, Ibbankatuwa Megalithic Tombs and Kalu diya Pokuna are a must see in this city.

Buddhist monks used to meditate here right from 3rd century BC. There is enough evidence that Tamil king Raja Raja Chola ruled Dambulla earlier known as Damballai. Dambulla is a world heritage site and UNESCO has marked it as a site for restoration and lighting.

Dambulla also has a sports stadium where world class matches takes place.

Kandalama reservoir is nearby. Sunset from here is a magnificent view.

Nuwara Eliya

Nuwara Eliya is famous for tea plantations. It is situated around 75 kilometers (47 miles approx) from Kandy. This place is also known as 'little England'. It is on top a hill that is famous for tree plantations. The weather is tropical yet the temperatures can go down to 0.4 degrees. Sri Lanka's tallest mountain Pidurutalagala known as Mount Pedro is here. Thick rain forests and tea plantations naturally give this area an ecological advantage.

Hakgala Botanical Gardens

The Hakgala Botanical Gardens is home to myriad hues of roses, ferns, unique flowers and trees. It also gives shelter to blue magpies and monkeys. Be careful with your belongings as monkeys may snatch them away.

Galways Land National Park

This is a haven for migratory birds including bulbuls and flycatchers. This place is densely forested and is nature's heaven on earth.

Lake Gregory

Boating, horse riding are some of the activities you can perform here. The cool waters surrounded by mountains are picturesque and you can click away to your satisfaction. It's an ideal place to take pictures.

Waterfalls

Nuwara Eliya has many waterfalls adding to the beauty and magnificence of the place. Devon Falls, Lover's Leap Waterfall, St. Clair's fall are some of them that attract tourists all around the year. It looks like heaven is showering its bountiful through these cascading waters.

National Parks

Victoria Park, Horton Plains National park is home to deer's and leopards, besides several other animals. Situated in a high altitude plateau it is a haven to animals, birds and thick forests. To the southwest, a trail climbs pyramid-shaped Adam's Peak, a pilgrimage place for several religions.

Nuwara Eliya golf club

Lush green wide expanse of plains enables this place to have one of the international golf clubs here.

Macwoods Tea Museum

Here you get to see how tea originated and how the British came to Sri Lanka just to take tea. The Museum is interesting and shows you in details exactly how tea is made and is home to rare quality of tea leaves.

Holy Trinity Church and Seetha Amman Temple

These are beautiful architecture and speak about the harmony of religions in Sri Lanka. The Hindus, Christians and Buddhists live in harmony here.

Moon plains safari (world's end)

You can see elephants in groups walking around while on a safari. Also this place is close to the sea and is the end of the world, literally speaking.

Trincomalee

Trincomalee is a port city on the northeast coast of Sri Lanka. It got its name from Tamil language where it was known as Thirukonamalai. The meaning is 'the lord's (thiru) corner (kona) mountain (malai)'. There is a Swami Rock cliff on which is perched the magnificent Koneswaram Temple. This was built by the Portuguese in the 17th century. From this temple cliff you can actually watch the blue whales playing in water. There is a huge statue of Shiva in the temple.

Nearby Gokanna Temple have panoramic views over the city and the coastline. Nilaveli Beach is a beautiful beach area where you just can chill for the day. It is one of the finest natural harbors in the world.

Badrakali Amman temple is another interesting place worth a visit. Trincomnalee is basically where the Sri Lankan Tamilians reside. Most of them are Hindus. You'll find several; Hindu temples here.

Till a decade ago Trincomalee was occupied by Tamil Elam militant group who were fighting to capture the place and have a separate state for themselves. The Sri Lankan government fought the separatists for 20 years before killing their supreme leader. Low key the fight is almost lost and peace has returned to the region.

Arugam Bay

Arugam Bay is situated in the south east coast of Sri Lanka. This is one of the best surfing points in Sri Lanka. You can enjoy water sports here. There are animal/ wild life sanctuaries here. The Yala National Park is home to giant elephants and the Kumana National Park houses deer's, lions, tigers and several other species that are rare to find anywhere else. The national animal of Sri Lanka is tiger.

Pasarichenai beach and Upali Beach are calm and peaceful places to enjoy a good swim. Arugam Bay is also well known for its night life. Beach parties are popular here with DJ's and beer and cocktails. You can hit the dance floor and then enjoy grilled food on the beach along with abundant liquor. Wining, dining and dancing can complete your vacation with fun and frolic. It is also known as surfer's paradise.

Activities to do in Sri Lanka
Enjoy a Cultural Dance

There are three traditional dance forms associated to Sri Lanka. Since Indian sub continent is close by, the Indian style is also fused into their culture. Kandayan dance is a form that is performed in the hill side known as Uda Rata Natum, Pahata Rata Natum in the southern part and Sabaragamuwa Natum in the northern and eastern parts of Sri Lanka. The three classical dance forms vary in style and movements.

South Indian cultural influence is largely visible in the culture of North Eastern Sri Lanka. Men and women are dressed in traditional attire with heavy jewelry. The Ruhunu dancers wear masks whereas Kandayan and Sabaragamu don't. Also the Ruhunu dance form is bold compared to the other two.

In Kandayan dance form only drum beats are important. The dancers move as per the drum beat. The beat is peppy and makes you also want to dance. It is upbeat and fun. If you're put up at a resort or hotel they'll arrange for an evening of dance show. Otherwise also you can enjoy a cultural evening at several halls across the cities.

Sightsee the Sigiriya Rock Fortress

Situated near Dambulla town is Sigiriya or Sinhagiri, an ancient rock fortress. The rock is 200 meters high and is ideal place to trek. It is known as the Pidurangala rock. Once you reach the top, the scenic beauty is spell bounding and mesmerizing. Enjoy the view from the top.

Another place to visit in Sigiriya is the archeological museum that is home to several rare artifacts from the by gone eras. You can learn about Sri Lankan art and history here. The sprawling museum is beautiful and offers a peak into Sri Lankan culture.

Mapagala fort is part of the Anuradhapura Empire built by King Kasyapa. It is located in the south of Sigiriya near the tank. The uniqueness of this fort is that it is built with uneven, hard rocks that are 20 meters in height.

Minneriya wild life park is a haven of elephants. If you wish to see the elephants then you should book with a tour guide. The jeep driver will know exactly what time the elephants will come and to which part of the park. It's an absolutely unforgettable experience. Sigiri safari is a must on your Sri Lankan visit.

Visit the Tea Plantation & Tea Factory

Sri Lanka exports more than $2 billion worth of tea every year. The country's GDP depends upon tea exports. It also employs more than a million workers in the tea industry. Right from plucking the tea leaves to drying and chafing and then packaging and transporting tea is the most lucrative business of Sri Lanka. Their green tea is world famous and has several health benefits.

Kandy, Nuwara Eliya and Dimbula are some of the hilly areas where tea plantations are. The weather conditions are conducive to grow tea here. You can visit the tea factory and see the varieties of tea grown here and also buy.

In the year 2737 BC the Chinese found how tea could be made from the leaves. Emperor Shen Nong who was also a scientist was sitting in the garden with a pot of boiling water when a leaf from the above tree fell into it and created fragrance. Also the color of the water changed. Intrigued he drank it and enjoyed the taste. He researched and found that the leaves had medicinal properties. History has it that tea originated from China, Tibet and Northern India.

The British when occupied India and Sri Lanka took tea drinking with them to the West. Also they wanted to balance the monopoly China was creating in Tea. Then tea entered Japan and they till today have a 'tea ceremony' that is followed like a ritual.

Visit the Strawberry Farms

Nuwara Eliya is where you find strawberry farms in Sri Lanka. The hilly region is favorable for strawberry cultivation. Ambewela Farm, Adam Agro, Rose Garden and many other farms located in Nuwara Eliya are famous for strawberry cultivation. You can actually see the rows of strawberry bushes with fruits hanging around. Ambewala and Ragala are two of the popular farms where the fruit is grown in open fields. They are around 30 minute drives from Spring Acre.

Strawberrys need careful protection from pests and diseases. They're housed in green houses and poly tunnels so that they're safe and protected from pests. Strawberry juice, jam and jelly are made at the nearby factories and are sold all over the country. They're even exported in a small scale. It'll be an interesting visit to this farm.

Polonnaruwa City Tour

Polonnaruwa is a cultural treasure of Sri Lanka. The ancient city was once in its glory during the rule of King Parakramabahu. The awe inspiring palace and its walls housed dagobas, temples and several other religious buildings and offered an atmosphere for religion to prosper. The old relics and architecture have been excavated and interesting facts have come to light about this glorious city.

Polonnaruwa is also known as the monkey kingdom. There are thousands of monkeys here. The palace's grandeur and structural masterpieces are the proud testimony of this. It is also believed that Lord Rama sent his monkey messenger to meet Sita and Ravana in Sri Lanka. You'll need a full day to visit each and every palace ruins and statues that stand testimony to the glory of ancient Sri Lanka.

Anuradhapura Sightseeing

Besides Sigiriya, Anuradhapura has several interesting places to visit. The well preserved ruins of ancient Sri Lankan civilization are there for you to see. Anuradhapura used to be the capital of old Sri Lanka and today is a hub for shopping, sightseeing and night life. Situated in the North Central Province of Sri Lanka, these are some of the important places to see.

Mihintale

Mihintale is a mountain peak near Anuradhapura in Sri Lanka. It is believed by Sri Lankans to be the site of a meeting between the Buddhist monk Mahinda and King Devanampiyatissa which inaugurated the presence of Buddhism in Sri Lanka.

The view is breathtaking and cool. You can enjoy hill top sight of Anuradhapura and nearby places. Sunset is a magnificent sight from here.

Isurumuniya

This is a Buddhist temple situated near the Tisa Tank in Anuradhapura. The temple looks charming very close to the lotus pond where there are carvings of elephants playing and splashing water. The significance of this temple is the carvings and statues that the earlier dynasty people have left behind. It is interesting to note that there is a stone carving of Isurumuniya lovers, elephant pond and also about the royal family. Through these carvings you get a peek into the lives of earlier Sri Lankans.

Ruwanvelisaya

The famous Bodhi tree is situated here. It is believed that Guathama Buddha achieved enlightenment under this tree. Ratna Prasada king's statue is carved in stone here. This dates back to 8th century.

Hakgala Botanical Gardens

Hakgala Botanical Gardens is one of the two best gardens in Sri Lanka. You find unusual flowers, fauna and are tastefully decorated. The sprawling campus is a sight for sore eyes. Usually Hakgala botanical garden closes by 5 PM. But on a full moon day it is open till 7 Pm to watch the moon rise. The entire garden is lit by shimmering moon light giving it an ethereal look. A trip to Nuwara Eliya is incomplete without visit to Hakgala Botanical Gardens. If you're a nature lover then you're sure to enjoy the trip to these gardens.

There are exotic blooms, flaming is myriad hues looking enchanting and delicate. The rose garden, orchid house, bulb garden are all carefully separated from each other. There are rare birds and species that enjoy a stay at this garden. A thick forest trail takes you into Hakgala Natural Reserve where you find animals like the Sloth Bear.

There is an entrance fee of LKR 1500.

Galle City Tour

Galle is situated in the south western tip of Colombo. It is famous for its fort. The majestic fort was built by the Portuguese and later maintained by the Dutch and British. You can see European architecture in the fort. This fort is a world heritage site marked by UNESCO. You'll find the Meera Mosqaue, All Saints Church and Hindu temple all inside the fort area. You can drive down this place. There are also cafes, restaurants to quench you thirst and snack on as well as shops, boutiques and art galleries for shopping unique art and artifacts. There is also Jet wing light house to see. There are several beach resorts that offer modern lifestyle near to the beach. You can live in luxury, comfort and enjoy beach life here. Era Beach, Amari Galle, The Bartizan Galle Fort to name a few has best views of the beach and food and drinks. These are boutique hotels that are available in affordable prices. Free Wi Fi, free breakfast is included in the price.

Water Sports in Unawatuna Beach

Unawatuna beach is the place where most of the water sports and adventure take place in Galle. It is filled with reservoirs, lakes, canals, rivers and lagoons. Calamander Unawatuna Beach is one of the finest places to stay. The hotel offers all modern facilities with a mini bar in your room, continental food, and two swimming pools for leisurely swim, one glass fronted lap pool that is one of a kind in Asia. There are also plush decks to relax and stretch with a large buffet and a la carte spread with a breathtaking ocean view.

Jungle beach is the best place for water sports. Surfing and Snorkeling are a must on your Sri Lankan vacation. You are offered leisure, aquatic sports, horseback riding, some exotic bird watching, and cultural tourism, sport tourism like hunting and scuba diving and eco tourism. You can tap your historic side by visiting the rich and enticing historic museums and you can soothe your soul and spirit with the enthralling and gorgeous natural sites and its sheer beauty.

The next best thing to getting married is a honeymoon in the stunning Sri Lankan shores. Couples will love walking over the soft, powdery sand, basking in the sun and relishing the breathtaking view. Tall palm trees fringed against sparkling deep blue seas set an ideal destination for a honeymoon couple in love. For the adventure lovers, diving or snorkeling in the crystal waters that reveal the magnificent marine worlds of reef fish, brilliantly colored corals and sea turtles can mesmerize you.

After a blissful day on the beach either romancing or experiencing the under water world, you can enjoy the night at the bustling casinos, night clubs and sing along with wandering beach bands. The foot tapping music comes predominantly from the African roots mixed with Indian country dance.

Budurugawala Rock Carvings

These are ancient rock carvings of Buddha that are more than 1000 years old. There are seven statues belonging to the Mahayana school of thought. This place is close to Ella.

Turtles Hatchery in Kosgoda

This place is unique in the sense that the staff from the hatchery wait in the night for the turtles to come to the shore and lay eggs. Once the job is done they go safely back into the sea leaving the eggs behind. The eggs are treated in the hatcheries.

Elephants &Wild Life Sanctuary

There is a bird sanctuary dedicated entirely to nature and among the very rare species, you can catch a glimpse of the turtle dove, white faced tropic bird and brush warbler to name a few.

Minneriya national park that lies at the northern edge is bestowed with natures' most spectacular lagoons and coral reefs and provides sheltered facilities for swimming, snorkeling and water sports all year round.

Sri Lanka may be a small island in the Indian Ocean yet has a lost of archeological sites, excavation and carvings to see. Their beaches are beautiful and unique. You can enjoy leisurely water sports, gorge on lip smacking cuisine and take pleasure on your vacation.

Buddhist Monasteries and Meditation Centers of Sri Lanka

There are hundreds of monasteries and meditation centers in Sri Lanka. If you're from the Western world then you're regarded with respect and dignity as you've the desire to learn about Dhamma. As a monk or wanting to learn about meditation you're welcome to stay for free at any of the monasteries.

Most of these monasteries and temples and meditation centers are in and around Anuradhapura, Colombo and Kandy.

Here is a list of monasteries that you can visit –

Amara Pura Nikaya

Asgiri Maha Viraya

Devanapatissa Vipassana Meditation Center

Island Hermitage

Kuragala

Mayura Pirivena is an ancient monastery in Anuradhapura.

Anuradhapura Maha Viharaya

Dhakshina Stupa

Na Uyana Aranya

Na Uyana Aranya is a meditation center amidst forest in the Dummiya mountain range. On the right side is the Pansiyagama section, on the center the 'Mountain' and on the left the Matale section. There is a cave to sit and meditate in peace. Also there is a huge hall in the first floor of the center for meditation. This monastery dates back to 3rd century BC. There is peace and tranquility here. This place is nearer to Dambulla.

Ritigala

This is a mountain range that has four peaks and is considered to be a natural reserve. There is an interesting story attached to this mountain peak. Hanuman, the monkey God who was the messenger of Lord Rama, sent to find his wife Sita arrived at this peak to look for her. From here he could see the forest where she was kept captive by Ravana. That place is now known as Seetha Eliya (where Sita lived). Later when Rama's brother was unconscious in the battle he sent Hanuman to fetch herbs and leaves that had medicinal qualities. Hanuman traveled over Ritigala with part of the Himalayan mountain range in hand and accidentally dropped a large piece of the mountain here at Ritigala. That is why the herbs and plants of a particular place in Ritigala have medicinal properties.

Nissarana Vanaya

This is one of the most respected monasteries in Sri Lanka. It is located in Mitirigala in the Western province close to the town of Kirindiwela. The monks live in separate huts and are dedicated to meditation practice. Meditation is done in a large meditation hall in the centre of the monastery.

It is interesting to note that in the morning monks go on alms begging to a kitchen area down the hill where lay-people who have cooked food donate it to them. A few monks go begging in the traditional style to the village. This is to keep them humble and modest and shed arrogance if there's any in them. The monks don't eat after mid-day.

In the evening there is a worship of the Bodhi Tree and Buddha followed by Pali chanting.

SriLankan Food

A holiday is never successful without good food and drinks; especially when you go on a beach vacation. Sri Lanka offers you the best of food and liquor to go with it. Local arrack is very popular here. Agriculture and farming are popular occupations in Sri Lanka. Rice is grown in abundance here. The locals eat rice as their staple food. Since the country is surrounded by water fish and sea food are popular here. The way it is prepared is different from the sea food you get in other parts of the world. Coconut is available in abundance here. Coconut milk is squeezed from the pulp and the fishes, prawns, sambal, star fish and crabs are all cooked in coconut milk. This gives a sweet taste along with the aromatic spices that are tangy. There are appams/ pancakes that are unique to this place. Rice flour is powdered and added with water and steamed on a mould. Having appam with stew is the staple breakfast for Sri Lankans. There are several street food stalls in all the beaches and cities of Sri Lanka. Enjoy street food here to taste local flavor. Hotels and resorts offer continental cuisine along with local recipes.

Ideal Meal

An ideal meal consists of rice, fish curry/ prawns, spicy dal, capsicum with pickled lime sambal, creamy potato curry complete the meal.

Pol Roti & Dal

This is flat bread made out of wheat, coconut paste and aromatic spices. Combined with lentil soup known as dal this makes an ideal breakfast or brunch.

Kottu Roti

The flat bread or roti is cut into pieces and eggs or prawns or meat is chopped and added to it. You can also add vegetables to the roti. This is ideal to eat as breakfast.

Drinks

Tea

Since Ceylon tea is world famous you can drink the best of tea here. In some places aromatic cardamom, ginger, lemon juice is added to tea to make it flavorful. Green tea is rich in anti oxidants and is good for weight loss and has other health benefits as well.

Coffee

Though Sri Lankans are tea drinkers, coffee used to be one of the favorite drinks in the 1800's. The Dutch and

British promoted coffee cultivation here. Now coffee is trying to make a come back. Starbucks cafes are there all around the country. The aromatic brew is something that should be relished when it is freshly ground.

Lion lager beer

One of the best selling beers in Sri Lanka, lion lager beer consists of 5% alcohol. It is the best thirst quencher.

Arrack

Ceylon Arrack is local liquor that is made out of coconut flowers that are hand picked and stored to age in casks. Arrack is a distilled alcoholic drink typically produced in the Indian subcontinent and Southeast Asia, made from the fermented sap of coconut flowers or sugarcane. It can also be made with rice or fruit depending upon the country of origin. The arrack produced in Sri Lanka is more refined and subtle compared to the Indian arrack.

Try these food and drinks on your vacation and complete your holiday totally satisfied and satiated.

Things to remember on Your Sri Lankan Visit

If you're travelling from the West then here are some things you need to know about Sri Lanka, its Culture and people's attitude. In Asian countries religion, tradition plays a vital role. People's lives are revolving around it. Sri Lanka has people from four religions living in harmony. Their main religion is Buddhism, then Hinduism, Christians and Islam. Main religions are Buddhism and Hinduism. They're traditional in nature. These are some of the things you need to remember on a sri Lankan vacation-

Wear decent clothes

People here wear full skirts with lose fitting blouses. Their traditional attire is a sari. This is a six meter cloth that is beautifully draped around the body accentuating the figure of a woman at the same time keeps her body covered from neck downwards. Do pack a one piece swim suit or else pack a sarong or a cloak to wear at the beach.

When you visit temples and monasteries wear fully covered clothes

like long skirt and blouse or pants and tops. Temples are places of worship and the people feel these places to be sacred. You cannot roam around in semi clad clothes. This might hurt the sentiments of Sri Lankans.

They're traditional and conservative

Sri Lanka was the first nation in the world to elect a female head of state, Sirimavo Bandaranaike. Sri Lankan society is matriarchal. Women dominate and run the family. Property gets transferred from mother to daughter. All the decisions are taken by women.

Don't hurt religious sentiments

Avoid talking about religious beliefs in Sri Lanka. People are steeped in religion, culture and they're God fearing people. Theravada Buddhism is the largest religion in Sri Lanka.

Mosquitoes and water born diseases

Don't forget to carry mosquito repellant with you. Apply it all the time. By evening hundreds will swarm your place of stay, if you aren't careful. Try to drink bottled water that is filtered and clean. Avoid drinking at road side cafes to avoid water born diseases like jaundice.

Plugs and sockets are not American style. Carry universal adapter to charge your phone & laptop.

Now that you've read the book go ahead and plan a vacation to Sri Lanka. The Tuk Tuk ride is a must on your holiday. It'll be a life time experience to travel in open air rickshaw. It's cheap as well as fun. Buses aren't helpful and taxis can be costly. Best is to live in a beach cottage, take the Tuk Tuk to see around the place and eat food at local restaurants. Most of the food is freshly made and hot. Tell them to make it less spicy for you. Finally enjoy a beautiful stay by the beach. Swim, surf, snorkel and gorge on sea food. Also take a look at the beautiful monasteries, temples and architecture of Sri Lanka that is steeped in history and has thousands of stories to tell. Take back wonderful memories, magnificent artifacts, healthy tea bags and a mind full of fantastic memories from your vacation to Sri Lanka.

Impressum & Haftungsausschluss

Impressum: 2019 Lilly Island

1. Auflage Alle Rechte, so weit nicht ausdrücklich anders gekennzeichnet, vorbehalten. Nachdruck, auch auszugsweise, verboten. Kein Teil dieses Werkes darf ohne schriftliche Genehmigung des Autors in irgendeiner Form reproduziert, vervielfältigt oder verbreitet werden.

2. Kontakt: Timo Schmid/

3. Covergestaltung: Lisa Biegemann

4. Coverfoto: Depositphoto

5.

6. Haftungsausschluss: Der Autor ist nicht haftbar für Verluste, die durch den Gebrauch dieser Informationen entstehen sollten. Der Inhalt dieses E-Books

repräsentiert die persönliche Erfahrung und Meinung des Autors und dient nur dem Unterhaltungszweck. Der Inhalt sollte nicht mit medizinischer Hilfe verwechselt werden. Die Nutzung dieses E-Books und die Umsetzung der darin enthaltenen Informationen, Anleitungen und Strategien erfolgen ausdrücklich auf eigenes Risiko. Der Autor kann für etwaige Unfälle und Schäden jeder Art, die sich bei der Umsetzung der in diesem Buch aufgeführten Tipps und Informationen ergeben, aus keinem Rechtsgrund eine Haftung übernehmen. Haftungsansprüche gegen den Autor für Schäden materieller oder ideeller Art, die durch die Nutzung oder Nichtnutzung der Informationen bzw. durch die Nutzung fehlerhafter und/oder unvollständiger Informationen verursacht

Solltest du nicht genau wissen, ob diese Tipps aus dem Ratgeber für dich geeignet sind, so nimm Kontakt zu deinem Arzt oder Apotheker auf. Für die Inhalte von den in diesem Buch abgedruckten Internetseiten sind ausschließlich die Betreiber der jeweiligen Internetseiten verantwortlich. Zum Zeitpunkt der Verlinkung wurde die jeweilige Webseite auf Vereinbarkeit mit deutschem Recht überprüft. Verstöße gegen geltendes Recht wurden nicht festgestellt. Bei den verlinkten Webseiten handelt es sich um Inhalte Dritter, für die der Autor nicht verantwortlich ist. Eine regelmäßige Überprüfung der verlinkten Webseiten auf Rechtmäßigkeit kann der Autor ausdrücklich nicht leisten. Der Autor hat keinen Einfluss auf Gestaltung und Inhalte fremder Internetseiten. Diesbezüglich distanzieren sich Autor und Verlag von allen fremden Inhalten. Zum Zeitpunkt der Verwendung waren keinerlei illegale Inhalte auf den Webseiten

117

irgendeiner Form für fehlerhafte Angaben und daraus entstandenen Folgen vom Verlag bzw. Autor übernommen werden. Solltest du nicht genau wissen, ob diese Tipps aus dem Ratgeber für dich geeignet sind, so nimm Kontakt zu deinem Arzt oder Apotheker auf. Für die Inhalte von den in diesem Buch abgedruckten Internetseiten sind ausschließlich die Betreiber der jeweiligen Internetseiten verantwortlich. Zum Zeitpunkt der Verlinkung wurde die jeweilige Webseite auf Vereinbarkeit mit deutschem Recht überprüft. Verstöße gegen geltendes Recht wurden nicht festgestellt. Bei den verlinkten Webseiten handelt es sich um Inhalte Dritter, für die der Autor nicht verantwortlich ist. Eine regelmäßige Überprüfung der verlinkten Webseiten auf Rechtmäßigkeit kann der

Kontakt: Timo Schmid

Münzweg 4

9500 Villach

11884978R00069

Made in the USA
Monee, IL
18 September 2019